Dinosaur Girl

CONTENTS

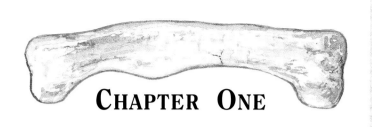

CHAPTER ONE

Holly stood by the stream, staring at the flickering reflection. Were her eyes deceiving her again?

She heard the snap of twigs and the thud of footsteps coming from behind her. She stepped forward, slipped, and fell into the stream.

It had all begun when Miss Stevens, Holly's teacher, told the class about Joan Wiffen, the "Dinosaur Woman."

Joan Wiffen had searched for dinosaur fossils in an area where experts thought dinosaurs had never lived. But she kept looking until she found dinosaur bones.

Then, everybody wanted to see them. Soon, Joan Wiffen was famous. She had believed in a dream and had continued to follow it.

Ever since she had heard of Joan Wiffen, Holly dreamed of finding dinosaur bones. And now she hoped today's school trip would make her dream come true.

Before the class left, Miss Stevens had grouped everyone into pairs.

"I'll go with Kate," said Holly. Kate and Holly always did things together.

"Not this time," said Miss Stevens. "I'll decide who you go with."

"But we're best friends," Holly and Kate said together.

"It's good to make new friends," the teacher replied. "Holly, you go with Leroy, and Kate, you go along with Amy."

Holly didn't think this was fair. Kate, however, didn't seem too sad. She was with Amy. And everyone wanted to be with Amy because Amy was good at everything and had everything. Now it looked like she even had Holly's best friend.

Holly was stuck with Leroy, and she was sure he wouldn't know anything about dinosaurs.

"Fossils," Leroy groaned as the bus started up. "Who cares about boring old fossils?"

"Fossils are not boring," Holly replied. "I think they're interesting, and I want to find one."

"Well, I bet you don't find anything," said Leroy. "There won't be any fossils to find. You can look on your own because I'm not going to help you."

Holly turned away and looked over at Kate and Amy, who were talking and laughing. Kate was enjoying herself too much to notice Holly. Holly felt miserable.

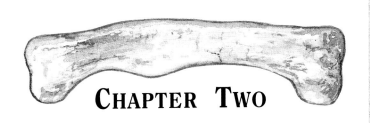

CHAPTER TWO

The bus stopped at a spot near the ocean. "We might as well take a break now," said Miss Stevens. "Off you go, and stay together," she said. "See what you can find on the seashore."

Holly headed straight for the sand dunes. Her dad had told her that, long ago, this area was covered by the ocean. Who knew what she might find buried there?

Holly looked around. There was so much sand. Where would she begin to look?

Holly knelt down and began to dig with her fingers. The hot sand burned her knees.

She could hear the class laughing as they raced the waves. But Holly didn't stop; she kept searching. "Joan Wiffen wouldn't give up," she said to herself, "and neither will I."

Suddenly, her fingers scraped against something. Excitedly, she tugged and pulled, releasing it with enough force to throw her back onto the sand.

She sat up and looked at her find. It was definitely old, and she was nearly sure it was a bone. Holly's heart was racing. Could it be a dinosaur bone?

Just then, a shadow fell across her, cutting out the sun. Holly turned and looked up to see Amy standing over her. "Amy," she said excitedly, "look what I just found! It's so big and old, it must be a dinosaur bone.

Do you think it is? Wait until I show it to everyone. Come on, we'll take it back together."

Amy bent down and snatched the bone from Holly's hand. "This isn't a dinosaur bone," she laughed. "It's probably an old leg bone from a cow. I can't wait to tell everyone!" She ran off, waving the bone in the air.

Holly followed Amy. "Of course it was a cow's bone!" Holly thought. She had wanted it to be a dinosaur bone so much, she'd talked herself into thinking it really was one.

Amy was the first to reach the others. Holly could hear her laughing as she waved the bone.

Leroy turned to look at Holly. "Did you really think that was from a dinosaur?" he asked.

"No kidding?" giggled Kate.

The whole class laughed, and even Miss Stevens smiled, although she tried to hide it.

Holly grabbed the bone from Amy and threw it into the sea.

"Dinosaur girl, dinosaur girl," chanted Amy. Some of the others joined in, too.

"That's enough," said Miss Stevens. "It's time to eat."

16

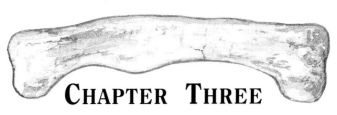

CHAPTER THREE

The class sat on the sand as they ate. Holly didn't talk to anybody. She felt as if she didn't have a single friend. She could see that Kate liked Amy better than her.

Once, Holly's dad had told her that when things get tough, you soon find out who your real friends are.

Holly knew her dad was right.

She stared out at the ocean, watching the waves breaking over one another, again and again.

She remembered Miss Stevens telling them that millions of years ago great creatures like mosasaurs and elasmosaurs filled the seas.

Their bones were sometimes found stuck in the cliffs near the ocean, and scientists studied these fossils to find out more about how the creatures had lived.

As the students finished their lunches, the bus driver walked over to Miss Stevens and said, "We've got a flat tire. I'll need time to fix it."

"OK, everybody," said Miss Stevens, "let's all walk to the cliff and back while we're waiting. But be careful."

Amy quickly ran to the front of the group, and Kate was right behind her. Holly stayed at the back, thinking about the cliff. She knew that fossils were sometimes found in sandstone.

Holly stared at the old, crumbly cliff. It looked like a piece of cheese with bites taken out where the sea had worn it away.

Amy raced past Holly on her way back from the cliff. She had a big fat smile on her face. Kate followed Amy, without ever looking at Holly.

Holly looked back at the cliff face. She thought she saw something sticking out of it. Her heart thumped loudly as she hurried over to the spot. Could it be a rib bone?

As Holly stretched out to grab ahold of it, Amy's voice called from behind her.

"Dinosaur girl, dinosaur girl, bones on the brain, and her head's in a whirl. It's just an old piece of driftwood," laughed Amy. "Tricked you, Holly!"

Holly stared at her. She was so angry, she could cry. But she wouldn't let Amy see that. She sped past Amy and started to walk back to the bus.

Kate caught her arm. "I'm sorry, Holly," she began. "That wasn't very funny. I told her not to do it."

Holly shook Kate's hand off her arm and kept on walking.

"Yeah, that was a mean trick," Leroy agreed. "That really wasn't funny at all."

Holly didn't reply, but she was happy to walk back to the bus with Leroy and sit next to him.

CHAPTER FOUR

"It's funny to think that there were once dinosaurs roaming all over the place," said Leroy as the bus started up. "They could have lived right here."

Holly liked having someone to talk to about dinosaurs. She told Leroy all she knew about the plant-eating diplodocus and the allosaurus, which ate meat.

She also knew about the spiky stegosaurus, the armor-plated ankylosaurus, and the mighty *Tyrannosaurus rex*.

Leroy knew about dinosaurs, too. He told Holly about the digs that took place in the old days.

"People would fight to keep the fossils they discovered," he said.

"They should have given the bones to museums for everyone to see," said Holly. "You're not supposed to keep them."

"I guess some people are just greedy," replied Leroy.

"We're here at last," Miss Stevens said. "Stay with your partners. We're running a little late, so don't wander too far, and don't go out of sight. We all need to meet back at the bus by two o'clock."

"Where do you think we should look?" asked Leroy. "It would be cool to find something."

"I don't really know where to start," Holly admitted.

"Well, let's go ahead and start at that bank by the stream," said Leroy.

"We'll begin at this end and work our way over to that tree."

Holly thought Leroy was getting the whole idea of hunting for fossils very quickly.

They searched carefully. Having Leroy made the search more fun, but they still didn't find what they were looking for.

Suddenly, one of the other boys shouted. "Hey, what's this? It looks like a shell."

Miss Stevens looked closely at the shell. "It's a marine fossil," she said.

"The ocean covered this entire valley at one time."

"Maybe we could find another one of those," Holly said to Leroy, pointing to the shell.

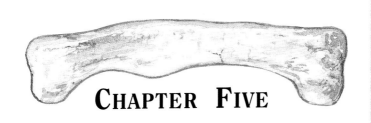

CHAPTER FIVE

Holly and Leroy set off ahead of the others, and walked farther along the stream. As they rounded the next bend, they startled two people who were examining a boulder beside the stream.

"What are you doing here?" the man asked.

"We're on a class trip, and we're looking for bones and fossils," replied Leroy. "What are you two doing here?"

The woman pushed up her mirrored sunglasses and laughed. "You could say we're looking for bones and fossils, too. Isn't that right, Rick?"

"Jan's right, we're doing a bit of fossil hunting, too," he said.

Holly didn't like the way they laughed at them. "Come on, Leroy," she said, "let's get going." She turned to walk up the stream.

"I didn't like the look of those two," said Holly.

"You can't always tell what people are like just by the way they look," said Leroy. "Do you want to go back and join the others and give up on our dinosaur hunt?"

Holly thought about it. It was starting to seem like a stupid hunt, really. She didn't think there was much chance of them ever finding anything.

Then Holly remembered Joan Wiffen, the "Dinosaur Woman." Now *she* wouldn't have given up.

"We've come this far," said Holly. "You can go back if you want, Leroy. I'm going to give it a little longer."

"Well," said Leroy, "if you're going on, I may as well go with you, too."

Holly was glad he said that.

They both pushed on along the streamside, stopping to look at anything that might be a bone.

Suddenly, Leroy remembered the time. "It's nearly two o'clock!" he yelled. "We'll have to hurry to get back to the bus on time."

Holly knew he was right. They would have to turn back.

Just as she turned, a chipped rock in the water caught her eye.

As she leaned down to take a closer look, she heard footsteps thumping up behind her.

"Look out!" shouted Leroy.

CHAPTER SIX

Holly knew exactly who would be behind her. It had to be the fossil hunters, and she wasn't going to let them get to whatever it was in the water. They would probably keep it for themselves or maybe even sell it.

She stepped forward for a closer look, slipped, and slid down the muddy bank and into the water.

Holly splashed around in the water, trying to stand up. She felt her hand close around a rock, and she held on to it tightly. Holly found she was clinging to the chipped rock she had seen before she had fallen into the water.

Her fingers traced the raised outline of what felt like a bone sticking out of the rock.

Holly looked up and saw the worried faces of Leroy, Kate, Amy, and the fossil hunters, Rick and Jan, who were all standing by the side of the stream, looking down at her.

They began shouting at once.

"Give me your hand," yelled Jan. "I'll pull you up."

"Hold on, I'm coming down to get you," said Rick.

"Look at that rock she's holding on to," shouted Amy. "I saw it first. I saw it first."

"Be quiet, Amy. Holly found it first," said Kate. "You're just jealous."

"Good for you, Holly. You did it," said Leroy, jumping up and down. "You found a fossil."

Rick slithered down the bank and helped Holly to her feet. And Jan scrambled down with a blanket to keep Holly warm.

Holly shivered with cold and excitement. She stared at the rock with the raised imprint of a bone. Was it just another one of her mistakes, or could it really be a dinosaur fossil this time?

Holly didn't know anymore.

Rick and Jan were studying the rock very carefully.

"Look at this, Jan!" cried Rick. "I don't believe it."

"Who would have ever thought it possible?" exclaimed Jan. "You certainly wouldn't expect to find something like this around these parts. This is such a lucky find. I can't wait to get this rock out of here and back to our lab for tests."

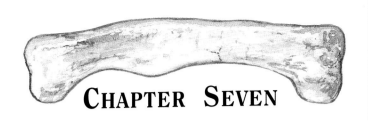

CHAPTER SEVEN

"What is it?" asked Kate.

"Well," Rick began, "We are paleontologists, people who study fossils. We heard that some fossils had been found in this area."

"So we thought," Jan continued, "we would take a look. Believe it or not, your friend here has stumbled on the fossil of a dinosaur's leg bone. We need to get it to some specialists to take a closer look, but I'm fairly sure it's an allosaurus."

"A dinosaur," said Kate. "Oh Holly, you've done it!"

Leroy's smile was so big, it just about stretched his ears out.

"You did it. You finally found one," he said, laughing.

"*We* did it," Holly corrected. "You were the one who kept me going."

She couldn't believe all this was really happening.

"Well, I could have found it," said Amy. "I nearly did."

"No you didn't, Amy," said Kate. "You weren't even close. Good for you, Holly."

The rest of the class arrived, shouting and waving.

"What did you find?" asked Miss Stevens. "We've been trying to catch up with you."

Rick turned to the teacher and explained who he and Jan were. "This girl has just found a genuine dinosaur fossil. A find like this will have the entire world sitting up and taking notice. It's amazing to find a bone like this, here. Everyone is going to be very excited when they hear about it."

"Hey, Holly, you did it! You're our own true dinosaur girl," one of her classmates yelled.

This time Holly didn't mind being called "dinosaur girl" – not one bit. She had followed her dream and found her dinosaur fossil.

Joan Wiffen, the Dinosaur Woman

Joan Wiffen was first called the Dinosaur Woman when she made an amazing discovery in a remote, wild area of New Zealand. In 1975, she found the first dinosaur fossil in New Zealand. It was a vertebra from a theropod dinosaur. Her discovery proved to paleontologists (people who study fossils) that dinosaurs had roamed that area. Joan's dream of finding dinosaur fossils helped paleontologists around the world find out more about how dinosaurs lived.

A fossil discovered in a rock

Joan Wiffen, in a remote area of New Zealand bush, helping to cut through a river boulder to get to the fossil inside

FROM THE AUTHOR

 I live with my family in a wonderful land full of rivers and beaches, mountains and valleys, and deep, dark forests. One day my younger son asked if there were ever any dinosaurs here. I understood why he would ask that. The whole place felt full of vast, ancient secrets. Why not dinosaurs?

So we did some research, and that's when we first heard about the "Dinosaur Woman." Everyone told her, "No way! dinosaurs never lived here." But Joan just kept asking, What if? and Why not? She had a dream, and she never stopped following it. Her dream gave me the idea for this story.

Susan Devereux

FROM THE ILLUSTRATOR

I live in Tauranga with my wife, Sue, and our three children, Chris, Ruth, and Stephen. All my life I have loved to draw, and my dream from a very young age was to be one of the best artists in the world.

It is very important to have dreams when you are young, and now I am helping other young people fulfill their dreams. I run workshops each year to teach children how to illustrate their own stories and books.

Bryan Pollard

Who Knows?

The Midnight Pig
PS I Love You, Gramps
Humphrey
Dinosaur Girl

The Dinosaur Connection
Myth or Mystery?
Hairy Little Critters
A Pocket Full of Posies

Written by **Susan Devereux**
Illustrated by **Bryan Pollard**
Photography by **Michael Schneider:** (p. 45);
Wellington Newspapers: (Joan Wiffen, p. 44)

05 04 03 02 01 00 99
10 9 8 7 6 5 4 3 2 1

Published in the United States by

a division of Reed Elsevier Inc.
500 Coventry Lane
Crystal Lake, IL 60014

Printed in Hong Kong
ISBN: 0-7901-1877-7